PUNCH LIBRARY OF HUMOUR

Edited by J. A. HAMMERTON

❧ Designed to provide in a series of volumes, each complete in itself, the cream of our national humour, contributed by the masters of comic draughtsmanship and the leading wits of the age to "Punch," from its beginning in 1841 to the present day ❧ ❧ ❧ ❧

MR. PUNCH IN THE HIGHLANDS

THRIFT

Highlander (he had struck his foot against a "stane"). "Phew-ts!—e-eh what a ding ma puir buit wad a gotten if a'd had it on!!"

MR. PUNCH IN THE HIGHLANDS

AS PICTURED BY

CHARLES KEENE, JOHN LEECH, GEORGE DU MAURIER, W. RALSTON, L. RAVEN-HILL, J. BERNARD PARTRIDGE, E. T. REED, G. D. ARMOUR, CECIL ALDIN, A S. BOYD, ETC.

WITH 140 ILLUSTRATIONS

PUBLISHED BY ARRANGEMENT WITH
THE PROPRIETORS OF "PUNCH"

🍃 🍃 🍃

THE EDUCATIONAL BOOK CO. LTD.

THE PUNCH LIBRARY OF HUMOUR

Twenty-five volumes, crown 8vo, 192 pages
fully illustrated

NORTHWARD HO!

SCOTSMEN — Highlanders and Low-landers—have furnished Mr. Punch with many of his happiest jokes. Despite the curious tradition which the Cockney imbibes with his mother's milk as to the sterility of Scotland in humour, the Scots are not only the cause of humour in others but there are occasions when they prove them-selves not entirely bereft of the faculty which, with his charming egoism, the Cockney supposes to be his own exclusive birthright. Indeed, we have it on the authority of Mr. Spielmann, the author of "The History of *Punch*," that "of the accepted jokes from unattached contributors (to *Punch*), it is a notable fact that at least 75 per cent. comes from north of the Tweed." As a very considerable proportion of these Scottish jokes make fun of the national characteristics of the Scot, it is clear that Donald has the supreme gift of being able to laugh at himself. It should be noted, however, that Mr. Punch's most celebrated Scottish joke ("Bang went saxpence"), which we give on page 153, was no invention, but merely the record of an actual conversation overheard by an Englishman!

In the present volume the purpose has been not so much to bring together a representative collection of the Scottish humour that has appeared in *Punch*, but to illustrate the intercourse of the "Sassenach" with the Highlander, chiefly as a visitor bent on sport, and incidentally to illustrate some of the humours of Highland life. Perhaps the distinction between Highlander and Lowlander has not been very rigidly kept, but that need trouble none but the pedants, who are notoriously lacking in the sense of humour, and by that token ought not to be peeping into these pages.

Of all Mr. Punch's contributors, we may say, without risk of being invidious, that Charles Keene was by far the happiest in the portrayal of Scottish character. His Highland types are perhaps somewhat closer to the life than his Lowlanders, but all are invariably touched off with the kindliest humour, and never in any way burlesqued. If his work overshadows that of the other humorous artists past and present represented in this volume, it is for the reason stated; yet it will be found that from the days of John Leech to those of Mr. Raven-Hill MR. PUNCH's artists have seldom been more happily inspired than when they have sought to depict Highland life and the lighter side of sport and travel north of the Tweed.

MR. PUNCH IN THE HIGHLANDS

SPORTING NOTES

THE following are the notes we have received from our Sporting Contributor. I wish we could say they were a fair equivalent for the notes he has received from *us*, to say nothing of that new Henry's patent double central-fire breech-loader, with all the latest improvements, and one of Mr. Benjamin's heather-mixture suits. Such as they are we print them, with the unsatisfactory consolation that if the notes are bad they are like the sport and the birds. Of all these it may be said that " bad is the best."

North and South Uist.—The awfully hard weather —the natives call it " soft " here—having rendered the chances of winged game out of the question, the sportsmen who have rented the shootings are glad to try the chances of the game, sitting, and have confined themselves to the whist from which the islands take their name. Being only two, they are reduced to double dummy. As the rental of the Uist Moors is £400, they find the points come rather high—so far.

Harris.—In spite of repeated inquiries, the pro- prietress of the island was not visible. Her friend, Mrs. Gamp, now here on a visit, declares she saw Mrs. H. very recently, but was quite unable to give me any information as to shootings, except the shootings of her own corns.

Fifeshire.—The renters of the Fife shootings generally have been seriously considering the feasibility of combining with those of the once well-stocked Drum Moor in Aberdeenshire, to get

ON THE HILLS

Deer Stalker (old hand, and fond of it). "Isn't it exciting? Keep cool!"
[*Jones isn't used to it, and, not having moved for the last half-hour, his excitement has worn off. He's wet through, and sinking fast in the boggy ground, and speechless with cold. So he doesn't answer.*

9

up something like a band—of hope, that a bag may be made some day. Thus far, the only bags made have been those of the proprietors of the shootings, who have bagged heavy rentals.

Rum.—I call the island a gross-misnomer, as there is nothing to drink in it but whiskey, which, with the adjacent " Egg," may be supposed to have given rise to the neighbouring " Mull "—hot drinks being the natural resource of both natives and visitors in such weather as we've had ever since I crossed the Tweed. I have seen one bird—at least so the gilly says—after six tumblers, but to me it had all the appearance of a brace.

Skye. – Birds wild. Sportsmen, ditto. Sky a gloomy grey—your correspondent and the milk at the hotel at Corrieverrieslushin alike sky-blue.

Cantire.—Can't you ? Try tramping the moors for eight hours after a pack of preternaturally old birds that know better than let you get within half a mile of their tails. Then see if you can't tire. I beg your pardon, but if you knew what it was to make jokes under my present circumstances, you'd give it up, or do worse. If I should not turn up shortly, and you hear of an inquest on a young

MR. BUGGLE'S FIRST STAG

1) AT THE FIRST SHOT
Mʳ BUGGLES FIRST STAG
LAY PRONE

2) ELATED WITH SUCCESS
Mʳ B. RUSHED UP
AND SEATED HIMSELF
ASTRIDE
HIS VICTIM

③ BUT ALAS IT WAS ONLY SLIGHTLY STUNNED, AND PROMPTLY ROSE TO THE OCCASION.

④ SO DID MR B

12

(5) THE LAW OF GRAVITY PROVED TOO STRONG WHEN A LUCKY SHOT FROM THE KEEPER

(6) PLACED MATTERS UPON A SATISFACTORY FOOTING ONCE MORE

man, in one of Benjamin's heather-mixture suits, with a Henry's central-fire breech-loader, and a roll of new notes in his possession, found hanging wet through, in his braces in some remote Highland shieling—break it gently to the family of

YOUR SPORTING CONTRIBUTOR.

A PIBROCH FOR BREAKFAST.

HECH, ho, the Highland laddie !
Hech, ho, the Finnon haddie !
Breeks awa',
Heck, the braw,
Ho, the bonnie tartan plaidie !
Hech, the laddie,
Ho, the haddie,
Hech, ho, the cummer's caddie,
Dinna forget
The bannocks het,
Gin ye luve your Highland laddie.

THE Member for Sark writes from the remote Highlands of Scotland, where he has been driving past an interminable series of lochs, to inquire where the keys are kept? He had better apply to the local authorities in the Isle of Man. They have a whole House of Keys. Possibly those the hon. Member is concerned about may be found among them.

MY ONLY SHOT AT A CORMORANT.

Here she comes!

There she goes!

FULL STOP IN THE DAWDLE FROM THE NORTH

(Leaves from the Highland Journal of Toby, M.P.)

" HERE'S a go," I said, turning to Sark, after carefully looking round the station to see if we really were back at Oban, having a quarter of an hour ago started (as we supposed) on our journey, already fifteen minutes late.

" Well, if you put it in that way," he said, " I should call it an entire absence of go. I thought it was a peculiarly jolting train. Never passed over so many points in the same time in my life."

" Looks as if we should miss train at Stirling," I remark, anxiously. " If so, we can't get on from Carlisle to Woodside to-night."

" Oh, that'll be all right," said Sark, airy to the last ; " we'll make it up as we go along."

Again sort of faint bluish light, which I had come to recognise as a smile, feebly flashed over

16

cadaverous countenance of the stranger in corner seat.

Certainly no hurry in getting off. More whistling, more waving of green flag. Observed that natives who had come to see friends off had quietly waited on platform. Train evidently expected back. Now it had returned they said good-bye over again to friends. Train deliberately steams out of station thirty-five minutes late. Every eight or ten miles stopped at roadside station. No one got in or got out. After waiting five or six minutes, to see if any one would change his mind, train crawled out again. Performance repeated few miles further on with same result.

" Don't put your head out of the window and ask questions," Sark remonstrated, as I banged down the window. " I never did it since I heard a story against himself John Bright used to tell with great glee. Travelling homeward one day in a particularly slow train, it stopped an unconscionably long time at Oldham. Finally, losing

" Where can that confounded fellow have got to with the lunch-basket ? "

all patience, he leaned out of the window, and in his most magisterial manner said, ' Is it intended that this train shall move on to-night?' The porter addressed, not knowing the great man, tartly replied, ' Put in thy big white yedd, and mebbe the train'll start.' "

Due at Loch Awe 1.32 ; half-past one when we strolled into Connel Ferry station, sixteen miles short of that point. Two more stations before we reach Loch Awe.

" Always heard it was a far cry to Loch Awe," said Sark, undauntedly determined to regard matters cheerfully.

Here he is, remarking, confidentially, that "that ginger-peer is apout the pest he ever tasted."

"You haven't come to the hill yet," said a sepulchral voice in the corner.

"What hill?" I asked.

"Oh, you'll see soon enough. It's where we usually get out and walk. If there are on board the train any chums of the guard or driver, they are expected to lend a shoulder to help the train up."

Ice once broken, stranger became communicative. Told us his melancholy story. Had been a W. S. in Edinburgh. Five years ago, still in prime of life, bought a house at Oban; obliged to go to Edinburgh once, sometimes twice, a week. Only thrice in all that time had train made junction with Edinburgh train at Stirling. Appetite failed; flesh fell away; spirits went down to water level. Through looking out of window on approaching Stirling, in hope of seeing South train waiting, eyes put on that gaze of strained anxiety that had puzzled me. Similarly habit contracted of involuntarily jerking up right hand with gesture designed to arrest departing train.

"Last week, coming north from Edinburgh," said the hapless passenger, " we were two hours late at Loch Awe. 'A little late to-day, aren't we?' I timidly observed to the guard. 'Ou aye! we're a bit late,' he said. 'Ye see, we had a lot of rams, and we couldna' get baith them and you up the hill; so we left ye at Tyndrum, and ran the rams through first, and then came back for ye.'"

Fifty minutes late at Killin Junction. So far from making up time lost at Oban, more lost at every wayside station.

"I hope we shan't miss the train at Stirling?" I anxiously inquired of guard.

Cockney Sportsman. " Haw — young woman, whose whiskies do you keep here?"

Highland Lassie. "We only keep McPherson's, sir."

C. S. "McPherson? Haw—who the deuce is McPherson?"

H. L. "My brother, sir."

During Mr. Spoffin's visit to the Highlands, he found a difficulty in approaching his game—so invented a method of simplifying matters. His "make-up," however, was so realistic, that the jealous old stag nearly finished him!

"Weel, no," said he, looking at his watch. "I dinna think ye'll hae managed that yet."

This spoken in soothing tones, warm from the kindly Scottish heart. Hadn't yet finally lost chance of missing train at Stirling that should enable us to keep our tryst at Woodside. But no need for despair. A little more dawdling and it would be done.

Done it was. When we reached Stirling, porters complacently announced English mail had left quarter of an hour ago. As for stationmaster, he

HIS IDEA OF IT

Native. "Is 't no **a** daft-like place this tae be takin' **a** view? There's no naething tae be seen for the trees. Noo, if ye was tae gang tae the tap o' Knockcreggan, that wad set ye fine! Ye can see *five coonties* frae there!"

was righteously indignant with inconsiderate travellers who showed disposition to lament their loss.

"Good night," said cadaverous fellow-passenger, feebly walking out of darkling station. "Hope you'll get a bed somewhere. Having been going up and down line for five years, I keep a bedroom close by. Cheaper in the end. I shall get on in the morning."

———

MERE INVENTION.—Up the Highlands way there is, in wet weather, a handsome cataract, the name whereof is spelt anyhow you like, but is pronounced "Fyres." There is not much water in hot weather, and then art assists nature, and a bucket or so of the fluid is thrown over for the delectation of tourists. One of them, observing this arrangement, said that the proprietor

"Began to pail his ineffectual Fyres."

[This story is quite false, which would be of no consequence, but that every Scottish tourist knows it to be false. Our contributor should really be more careful.]

TOURING IN THE HIGHLANDS

" Hullo, Sandy ! Why haven't you cleaned my carriage, as I told you last night ? "

" Hech, sir, what for would it need washing ? It will be just the same when you'll be using it again ! "

FROM OUR BILIOUS CONTRIBUTOR

To MR. PUNCH.

MY DEAR SIR,*

Embarking at Bannavie very early in the morning—*diluculo surgere saluberrimum est*, but it is also particularly disagreeable—I was upon the canal of the Caledonians, on my way to the capital of the Highlands. This is the last voyage which, upon this occasion, I shall have the pleasure of describing. The vessel was commanded by Captain Turner, who is a remarkable meteorologist, and has emitted some wonderful weather prophecies. Having had, moreover, much opportunity of observing character, in his capacity of captain of boats chiefly used by tourists, he is well acquainted with the inmost nature of the aristocracy and their imitators. Being myself of an aristo-

---

* We perfectly understand this advance towards civility as the writer approaches the end of his journey. He is a superior kind of young man, if not the genius he imagines himself.—*Ed.*

cratic turn of mind (as well as shape of body) it was refreshing to me to sit with him on the bridge and speak of our titled friends.

Fort Augustus, which we passed, is not called so from having been built by the Roman Emperor of that name, quite the reverse. The next object of interest is a thing called the Fall of Foyers, which latter word is sounded like fires, and the announcement to Cockneys that they are going to see the affair, leads them to expect something of a pyrotechnic character. It is nothing of that sort. The steamboat is moored, you rush on shore, and are instantly arrested by several pikemen—I do not mean soldiers of a mediæval date, but fellows at a gate, who demand fourpence apiece from everybody landing in those parts. Being in Scotland, this naturally made me think I had come to Johnny Groat's house, but no such thing, and I have no idea of the reason of this highway robbery, or why a very dirty card should have been forced upon me in proof that I had submitted. We were told to go up an ascending road, and then to climb a dreadfully steep hill, and that then we should see something. For my own part, I felt inclined

A PLEASANT PROSPECT!

English Tourist. "I say, look here. How far is it to this Glenstarvit? They told us it was only——" *Native.* "Aboot four miles." *Tourist (aghast).* "All bog like this?" *Native.* "Eh—h—this is just naethin' till't!!"

to see everybody blowed first, but being over-persuaded, I saw everybody blowed afterwards, for that hill is a breather, I can tell you. However, I rushed up like a mounting deer, and when at the top was told to run a little way down again. I did, and saw the sight. You have seen the cataracts of the Nile? It's not like them. You have seen a cataract in a party's eye. It's not like that. Foyers is a very fine waterfall, and worthy of much better verses than some which Mr. Burns addressed to it in his English style, which is vile. Still, the waterfall at the Colosseum, Regent's Park, is a good one, and has this advantage, that you can sit in a chair and look at it as long as you like, whereas you walk a mile to Foyers, goaded by the sailors from the vessel, who are perpetually telling you to make haste, and you are allowed about three minutes and fourteen seconds to gaze upon the scene, when the sailors begin to goad you back again, frightening you with hints that the captain will depart without you. Precious hot you come on board, with a recollection of a mass of foam falling into an abyss. That is not the way to see Foyers, and I hereby advise

ANOTHER MISUNDERSTANDING

'Arry (on a Northern tour, with Cockney pronunciation).
"Then I'll 'ave a bottle of aile."

Hostess of the Village Inn. "*Ile*, sir? We've nane in the hoose, but castor ile or paraffin. Wad ony o' them dae, sir?"

all tourists who are going to stop at Inverness, to drive over from thence, take their time at the noble sight, and do the pier-beggars out of their fourpences.

The stately towers of the capital of the Highlands are seen on our right. A few minutes more, and we are moored. Friendly voices hail us, and also hail a vehicle. We are borne away. There is news for us. We are forthwith—even in that carriage, were it possible—to induct ourselves into the black tr × ws × rs of refined life and the white cravat of graceful sociality, and to accompany our host to the dinner of the Highland railwaymen. *We* rail. We have not come six hundred miles to dress for dinner. Our host is of a different opinion, and being a host in himself, conquers our single-handed resistance. We attend the dinner, and find ourselves among Highland chieftains plaided and plumed in their " tartan array." (Why doesn't Horatio MacCulloch, noble artist and Highland-man, come to London and be *our* tartan R.A.?) We hear wonders of the new line, which is to save folks the trouble of visiting the lost tribe at Aberdeen, and is to take them direct from Inverness to

THE WEIRD SISTERS

Perth, through wonderful scenery. We see a programme of toasts, to the number of thirty-four,
which of course involves sixty-eight speeches.
There is also much music by the volunteers—not,
happily, by bag-pipers. We calculate, on the
whole, that the proceedings will be over about four
in the morning. Ha! ha! *Dremacky*. There is a
deus ex machinâ literally, a driver on an engine,
and he starts at ten. Numbers of the guests
must go with him. *Claymore!* We slash out the
toasts without mercy—without mercy on men set
down to speak and who have spoiled their dinner
by thinking over their *impromptus*. But there is
one toast which shall be honoured, yea, with the
Highland honours. *Mr. Punch's* health is proposed. It is well that this handsome hall is
built strongly, or the Highland maidens should
dance here no more. The shout goes up for
Mr. Punch.

I believe that I have mentioned to you, once or
twice, that I am an admirable speaker, but upon
this occasion I surpassed myself—I was in fact,
as the Covent Garden play-bills say, "unsur-
passingly successful." Your interests were safe

DEER-STALKING MADE EASY

The patent silent motor-crawler.

c

in my hands. I believe that no person present heard a syllable of what I said. It was this:

[It may have been, but as what our correspondent has been pleased to send as his speech would occupy four columns, we prefer to leave it to immortality in the excellent newspaper of which he sends us a " cutting." We incline to think that he *was* weak enough to say what he says he said, because he could not have invented and written it out after a Highland dinner, and it was published next morning. It is extremely egotistical, and not in the least entertaining —*Ed.*]

Among the guests was a gentleman who owns the mare who will certainly win the Cesarewitch. *I know this for a fact*, and I advise you to put your money on *Lioness*. His health was proposed, and he returned thanks with the soul of wit. I hope

ILLUSTRATED QUOTATIONS

(*One so seldom finds an Artist who realises the poetic conception.*)

" Is this the noble Moor . . . ?"—*Othello*, Act IV., Scene 1.

DRACONIAN

SCENE.—*Police Court, North Highlands.*

Accused. " Put, Pailie, it's na provit ! "

Bailie. " Hoot toots, Tonal, and hear me speak ! Aw'll only fine ye ha'f-a-croon the day, because et's no varra well provit. But if ever ye come before me again, ye'll no get aff under five shillin's, whether et's provit or no ! ! "

MANNERS AND CUSTOMS OF YE ENGLYSHE
IN 1849

DEERE STALKYNGE IN YE HYGHLANDES

he recollects the hope expressed by the proposer touching a certain saddling-bell. I thought it rather strong in "Bible-loving Scotland," but to be sure, we were in the Highlands, which are England, or at all events where the best English spoken in Scotland is heard.

We reached our house at an early hour, and I was lulled to a gentle slumber by the sound of the river Ness. This comes out of Loch Ness, and in the latest geographical work with which I am acquainted, namely, "Geography Anatomiz'd, by Pat. Gordon, M.A.F.R.S. Printed for Andr. Bell, at the Cross Keys and Bible in Cornhill, and R. Smith, under the Royal Exchange, 1711," I read that "towards the north-west part of *Murray* is the famous *Lough-Ness* which never freezeth, but retaineth its natural heat, even in the extremest cold of winter, and in many places this lake hath been sounded with a line of 500 fathom, but no bottom can be found" (just as in the last rehearsal

ONE OF THE ADVANTAGES OF SHOOTING
FROM A BUTT

Keeper (on moor rented by the latest South African millionaire, to guest). "Never mind the birds, sir. For onny sake, lie down! The maister's gawn tae shoot!"

39

of the artisans' play in the *Midsummer Night's Dream*), but I believe that recent experiments have been more successful, and that though no lead plummet would go so deep, a volume by a very particular friend of mine was fastened to the line, and descended to the bottom in no time. I will mention his name if he is not kind to my next work, but at present I have the highest esteem and respect for him. I only show him that I know this little anecdote.

There were what are called Highland games to be solemnised in Inverness. I resolved to attend them, and, if I saw fit, to join in them. But I was informed by a Highland friend of mine, Laidle of Toddie, a laird much respected, that all competitors must appear in the kilt. As my own graceful proportions would look equally well in any costume, this presented no difficulty, and I marched off to Mr. Macdougall, the great Highland costumier, and after walking through a dazzling array of Gaelic glories, I said, mildly,

" Can you make me a Highland dress ? "

"Certainly, in a few hours," said Mr. Macdougall ; but somehow I fancied that he did not seem to

THE TWELFTH

(Guilderstein in the Highlands)

Guild. (his first experience). " I've been swindled! That confounded agent said it was all drivin' on this moor, and look at it, all hills and slosh! Not a decent carriage road within ten miles!"

think that I was displaying any vast amount of sense.

"Then, please to make me one, very handsome," said I ; "and send it home to-night." And I was going out of the warehouse.

"But, sir," said Mr. Macdougall, "do you belong to any clan, or what tartan will you have ?"

"Mr. Macdougall," said I, " it may be that I do belong to a clan, or am affiliated to one. It may be, that like Edward Waverley, I shall be known hereafter as the friend of the sons (and daughters) of the clan ———. It may be that if war broke out between that clan and another, I would shout our war-cry, and, drawing my claymore, would walk into the hostile clan like one o'clock. But at present that is a secret, and I wear not the garb of any clan in particular. Please to make me up a costume out of the garbs of several clans, but be sure you put the brightest colours, as they suit my complexion."

I am bound to say that though Mr. Macdougall firmly declined being party to this arrangement, which he said would be inartistic, he did so with the utmost courtesy. My opinion is, that he

THE MATERNAL INSTINCT

The Master. "I'm sayin', wumman, ha'e ye gotten the tickets?"
The Mistress. "Tuts, haud your tongue aboot tickets. Let me count the weans!"

thought I was a little cracked. Many persons have thought that, but there is no foundation for the suspicion.

"You see, Mr. Macdougall," says I, "I am a Plantagenet by descent, and one of my ancestors was hanged in the time of George the Second. Do those facts suggest anything to you in the way of costume ?"

"The first does not," he said, "but the second may. A good many persons had the misfortune to be hanged about the time you mention, and for the same reason. I suppose your ancestor died for the Stuarts."

"No, sir, he died for a steward. The unfortunate nobleman was most iniquitously destroyed for shooting a plebeian of the name of Johnson, for which reason I hate everybody of that name, from Ben downwards, and will not have a Johnson's *Dictionary* in my house."

"Then, sir," says Mr. Macdougall, "the case is clear. You can mark your sense of the conduct of the sovereign who executed your respected relative. You can assume the costume of his chief enemies. You can wear the Stuart tartan."

44

"NEMO ME IMPUNE," &c.   TIPPED l

The Irrepressible. "Hi, Scotty, tip us the 'Ighland fling."

"Hm," says I. "I should look well in it, no doubt ; but then I have no hostility to the present House of Brunswick."

"Why," says he, laughing ; "Her Majesty dresses her own princes in the Stuart tartan. *I* ought to know that."

"Then that's settled," I replied.

Ha! You would indeed have been proud of your contributor, had you seen him splendidly arrayed in that gorgeous garb, and treading the heather of Inverness High Street like a young mountaineer. He did not look then like

EPICURUS ROTUNDUS.

Inverness Castle.

———

NOTICE TO THE HIGHLANDERS.—Whereas Mr. Punch, through his "Bilious Contributor," did on the 7th November, 1863, offer a prize of fifty guineas to the best Highland player at Spellikins, in the games for 1873. And whereas Mr. Punch has had the money, with ten years' interest, quite ready, and waiting to be claimed. And whereas no Highland player at Spellikins appeared at the games of 1873. This to give notice that Mr. Punch

Return of the wounded and missing Popplewitz omitted to
send in after his day on the moors.

has irrevocably confiscated the money to his own sole and peculiar use, and intends to use it in bribery at the next general election. He begs to remark to the Highlands, in the words of his ancestor, Robert Bruce, at Bannockburn—"There is a rose fallen from your wreath!"*

PUNCH.

7th November, 1873.

* Of course the King said nothing so sweetly sentimental. What he did say to Earl Randolph was, "Mind your eye, you great stupid ass, or you'll have the English spears in your back directly." Nor did the Earl reply, "My wreath shall bloom, or life shall fade. Follow, my household!" but, with an amazing great curse, "I'll cook 'em. Come on, you dawdling beggars, and fulfil the prophecies!" But so history is written.

———

MORE REVENGE FOR FLODDEN.—*Scene : a Scotch Hotel. Tourist (indignant at his bill).* "Why, landlord, there must be some mistake there!" *Landlord.* "Mistake? Aye, aye. That stupid fellow, the waiter, has just charged you five shillings—too little."

———

FROM THE MOORS.—*Sportsman.* "Much rain Donald?" *Donald.* "A bit soft. Just wet a' day, wi' showers between."

48

RECRIMINATION

Inhabitant of Uist. " I say, they'll pe speaking fa-ar petter English in Uist than in Styornaway."

Lass of the Lewis. " Put in Styornaway they'll not pe caa-in' fush ' feesh,' whatefer ! "

THE HIGHLAND GAMES AT MACJIGGITY

WHILST staying at MacFoozle Castle, my excellent host insisted that I should accompany him to see the Highland games. The MacFoozle himself is a typical Hielander, and appeared in

GUILDERSTEIN IN THE HIGHLANDS

Guilderstein. " Missed again ! And dat fellow, Hoggen-heimer, comin' on Monday, too! Why did not I wire to Leadenhall for an 'aunch, as Betty told me!"

Juvenis. "Jolly day we had last week at McFoggarty's wedding! Capital champagne he gave us, and we did it justice, I can tell you——"

Senex (who prefers whiskey). "Eh—h, mun, it's a' vera weel weddings at ye-er time o' life. Gie me a gude solid funeral!"

a kilt and jelly-bag—philabeg, I mean. Suggested to him that I should go, attired in pair of bathing-drawers, Norfolk jacket, and Glengarry cap, but he, for some inscrutable reason of his own, negatived the idea. Had half a mind to dress in kilt myself, but finally decided against the national costume as being too draughty.

Arrived on ground, and found that "tossing the
caber" was in full progress. Braw laddies
struggled, in turn, with enormous tree trunk.
The idea of the contest is, that whoever succeeds
in killing the greatest number of spectators by
hurling the tree on to them, wins the prize.
Fancy these laddies had been hung too long, or
else they were particularly braw. Moved up to
windward of them promptly.

" Who is the truculent-looking villain with red
whiskers ? " I ask.

" Hush ! " says my host, in awed tones. " That
is the MacGinger himself! "

I grovel. Not that I have ever even heard his
name before, but I don't want to show my ignor-
ance before the MacFoozle. The competition
of pipers was next in order, and I took to my
heels and fled. Rejoined MacFoozle half an hour
later to witness the dancing. On a large raised
platform sat the judges, with the mighty Mac-
Ginger himself at their head. Can't quite make
out whether the dance is a Reel, a Strathspey, a
Haggis, or a Skirl—sure it is one or the other.
Just as I ask for information, amid a confusing

HEBRIDEAN SPORT

Shooting Tenant (accounting for very large species of grouse which his setter has just flushed). "Capercailzie! By George!"

Under-keeper Neil. "I'm after thinking, sir, you'll have killed Widow McSwan's cochin cock. Ye see the crofters were forced to put him and the hens away out here till the oats is ripe!"

whirl of arms and legs and "Hoots!" a terrific crack is heard, and the platform, as though protesting at the indignities heaped upon it, suddenly gives way, and in a moment, dancers, pipers, and judges are hurled in a confused and struggling heap to the ground. The MacGinger falls upon some bag-pipes, which emit dismal groanings beneath his massive weight. This ends the dancing prematurely, and a notice is immediately put up all round the grounds that (to take its place) "There will be another competition of bag-pipes." I read it, evaded the MacFoozle, and fled.

SONG FOR A SCOTCH DUKE.

My harts in the Highlands shall have their hills clear,
My harts in the Highlands no serf shall come near—
I'll chase out the Gael to make room for the roe,
My harts in the Highlands were ever his foe.

THINGS NO HIGHLANDER CAN UNDERSTAND.
Breaches of promise.

LATEST FROM THE MOORS

Intelligent Foreigner. **"Tell me—zee 'Ilanders, do zay always wear zee raw legs?"**

A GROAN FROM A GILLIE

Lasses shouldna' gang to shoot,
> Na, na!

Gillies canna' help but hoot,
> Ha, ha!

Yon douce bodies arena' fittin'
Wi' the gudeman's to be pittin',
Bide at hame and mind yere knittin'!
> Hoot, awa'!

"Wimmen's Rechts" is vara weel,
> Ooh, aye!

For hizzies wha've nae hearts to feel;
> Forbye

Wimmen's Rechts is aiblins Wrang
When nat'ral weak maun ape the strang,

56

An' chaney cups wi' cau'drons gang,
Auch, fie!
Hennies shouldna' try to craw
Sae fast—
Their westlin' thrapples canna' blair
Sic a blast.
Leave to men-folk bogs and ferns,
An' pairtricks, muircocks, braes, and cairns;
And lasses! ye may mind the bairns—
That's best!

TONALT (X) his mark.

A PRECISIAN

Artist (affably). "Fine morning." *Native.* "No' bad ava'."
Artist. "Pretty scenery." *Native.* "Gey an' good."
Artist (pointing to St. Bannoch's, in the distance). "What place is that down at the bottom of the loch?"
Native. "It's no at the bottom—it's at the fut!"
Artist (to himself). "You past-participled Highlander!"
[Drops the subject!

57

THE THING TO DO IN SCOTLAND

(More Leaves from the Highland Journal of Toby, M.P.)

Quiverfield, Haddingtonshire, Monday.—You can't spend twenty-four hours at Quiverfield without having borne in upon you the truth that the only thing to do in Scotland is to play goff. (On other side of Tweed they call it golf. Here we are too much in a hurry to get at the game to spend time on unnecessary consonant.) The waters of what Victor Hugo called " The First of the Fourth" lave the links at Quiverfield. Blue as the Mediterranean they have been in a marvellous autumn, soon to lapse into November. We can see the Bass Rock from the eighth hole, and can almost hear the whirr of the balls skimming with swallow flight over the links at North Berwick.

Prince Arthur here to-day, looking fully ten years younger than when I last saw him at Westminster. Plays through live-long day, and drives off fourteen miles for dinner at Whittinghame, thinking no more of it than if he were crossing

THE "IRREPRESSIBLE" AGAIN

Gent in Knickerbockers. "Rummy speakers them 'Ighlanders, 'Enery. When we wos talking to one of the 'ands, did you notice 'im saying '*nozzing*' for '*nothink*,' and '*she*' for '*'e*,'?"

Palace Yard. Our host, Waverley Pen, is happy
in possession of links at his park gates. All his
own, for self and friends. You step through the
shrubbery, and there are the far-reaching links ;
beyond them the gleaming waters of the Forth.
Stroll out immediately after breakfast to meet the
attendant caddies ; play goff till half-past one ;
reluctantly break off for luncheon ; go back
to complete the
fearsome four-
some ; have tea
brought out to
save time ; leave
off in bare time
to dress for
dinner; talk goff
at dinner ; ar-
range matches
after dinner;
and the new
morning finds
the caddies
waiting as be-
fore.

Fingen's finger.

"THE LAST STRAW"

"Tired out, are you?   Try a drop of brandy!   Eh!—what!—confound—
By jingo, I've forgotten my flask!"

Decidedly the only thing to do in Scotland is to play goff.

Deeside, Aberdeenshire, Wednesday.—Fingen, M.P., once told an abashed House of Commons that he " owned a mountain in Scotland." Find, on visiting him in his ancestral home, that he owns a whole range. Go up one or two of them ; that comparatively easy ; difficulty presents itself when we try to get down. Man and boy, Fingen has lived here fifty years ; has not yet acquired know-ledge necessary to guide a party home after ascend-ing one of his mountains. Walking up in cool of afternoon, we usually get home sore-footed and hungry about midnight.

" Must be going now," says Fingen, M.P., when we have seen view from top of mountain. "Just time to get down before dark. But I know short cut ; be there in a jiffy. Come along."

We come along. At end of twenty minutes find ourselves in front of impassable gorge.

" Ha ! " says Fingen, M.P., cheerily. "Must have taken wrong turn ; better go back and start again."

All very well to say go back ; but where were

NOTHING LIKE MOUNTAIN AIR

Tourist (who has been refreshing himself with the toddy of the country). "I shay, ole fler! Highlands seem to 'gree with you wonerfly—annomishtake. Why, you look DOUBLE the man already!"

we ? Fingen, M.P., knows ; wets his finger ; holds
it up.

" Ha !" he says, with increased joyousness of
manner; "the wind is blowing that way, is it ?
Then we turn to the left."

Another twenty minutes stumbling through aged
heather. Path trends downwards.

" That's all right," says Fingen, M.P. ; " must
lead on to the road."

Instead of which we nearly fall into a bubbling
burn. Go back again ; make bee line up acclivity
nearly as steep as side of house; find ourselves
again on top of mountain.

" How lucky !" shouts Fingen, M.P., beaming
with delight.

As if we had been trying all this time to get to
top of mountain instead of to bottom !

Wants to wet his finger again and try how the
wind lies. We protest. Let us be saved that at
least. Fingen leads off in quite another direction.
By rocky pathway which threatens sprains; through
bushes and brambles that tear the clothes ; by
dangerous leaps from rock to rock he brings us to
apparently impenetrable hedge. We stare forlorn.

64

THE HEIGHT OF BLISS

Highland Shepherd. " Fine toon, Glasco', I pelieve, and lots o' coot meat there."

Tourist. " Oh, yes, lots."

Highland Shepherd. " An' drink, too ? "

Tourist. " Oh, yes."

Highland Shebherd (doubtingly). " Ye'll get **porter tae yir** parrich ? "

Tourist. " Yes, if we like."

Highland Shepherd. " Cra-ci-ous ! "

[*Speechless **with admiration.***

The crack of the whip('s pate!)

"Ha!" says Fingen, M.P., more aggressively cheerful than ever. "The road is on other side. Thought we would come upon it somewhere." Somehow or other we crawl through.

"Nothing like having an eye to the lay of country," says Fingen, M.P., as we limp along the road. "It's a sort of instinct, you know. If I hadn't been with you, you might have had to camp out all night on the mountain."

They don't play goff at Deeside. They bicycle. Down the long avenue with spreading elm trees deftly trained to make triumphal arches, the bicycles come and go. Whipsroom, M.P., thinks

TENACITY

First North Briton (*on the Oban boat, in a rolling sea and dirty weather*). " Thraw it up, man, and ye'll feel a' the better !"

Second ditto (*keeping it down*). " Hech, mon, it's whuskey !! "

opportunity convenient for acquiring the art of cycling. W. is got up with consummate art. Has had his trousers cut short at knee in order to display ribbed stockings of rainbow hue. Loose tweed-jacket, blood-red necktie, white felt hat with rim turned down all round, combine to lend him air of a Drury Lane bandit out of work. Determined to learn to ride the bicycle, but spends most of the day on his hands and knees, or on his back. Looking down avenue at any moment pretty sure to find W. either running into the iron fence, coming off sideways, or bolting head first over the handles of his bike. Get quite new views of him fore-shortened in all possible ways, some that would be impossible to any but a man of his determination.

" Never had a man stay in the house," says Fingen, M.P., ruefully, " who so cut up the lawn with his head, or indented the gravel with his elbows and his knees."

Evidently I was mistaken about goff. Cycling's the thing in Scotland.

Goasyoucan, *Inverness-shire*, *Saturday*.—Wrong again. Not goff nor cycling is the thing to do in

EXCUSABLE WRATH

Drover (exhausted with his struggles). "Whit are ye wouf, woufan' there, ye stupit ass! It wud be wis-eer like if ye gang awn hame, an' bring a barrow!"

A SOFT IMPEACHMENT

Sporting Saxon (mournfully, after three weeks' incessant down-pour). "Does it always rain like this up here, Mr. McFuskey?"

His Guide, Philosopher, and Friendly Landlord (calmly). "Oo aye, it's a-ye just a wee bit shooery."!!

Scotland. It's stalking. Soon learn that great truth at Goasyoucan. The hills that encircle the house densely populated with stags. To-day three guns grassed nine, one a royal. This the place to spend a happy day, crouching down among the heather awaiting the fortuitous moment. Weather no object. Rain or snow out you go, submissive to guidance and instruction of keeper; by comparison with whose tyranny life of the ancient galley-slave was perfect freedom.

ANTIQUARIAN RESEARCH

2 A.M.

Brown (who has taken a shooting-box in the Highlands, and has been " celebrating " his first appearance in a kilt). "Worsht of these ole-fashioned beshteads is, they take such a lot of climbin' into!"

Consummation of human delight this, to lie prone on your face amid the wet heather, with the rain pattering down incessantly, or the snow pitilessly falling, covering you up flake by flake as if it were a robin and you a babe in the wood. Mustn't stir ; mustn't speak ; if you can conveniently dispense with the operation, better not breathe. Sometimes, after morning and greater part of

GUILDERSTEIN IN THE HIGHLANDS

Mrs. G. " We must leave this horrible place, dear. The keeper has just told me there is disease on the moor. Good gracious, the boys might take it ! "

A GREAT DRAWBACK

Dougal (with all his native contempt for the Londoner). " Aye,
mon, an' he's no a bad shot ? "
   Davie. " 'Deed an' he's a verra *guid* shot."
   Dougal. " Hech ! it's an awfu' peetie he's a **Londoner !** "

afternoon thus cheerfully spent, you may get a
shot; even a stag. Also you may not; or, having
attained the first, may miss the latter. At any
rate you have spent a day of exhilarating
delight.

   Stalking is evidently the thing to do in Scotland.
It's a far cry to the Highlands. Happily there is
Arthur's Seat by Edinburgh town where beginners
can practise, and old hands may feign delight of
early triumphs.

NOTES FROM THE HIGHLANDS

" Jam satis terris," &c.

Alt-na-blashy. — The aqueous and igneous agencies seem to be combined in these quarters, for since the rain we hear of a great increase of burns. In default of the moors we fall back on the kitchen and the cellar. I need hardly add that dry wines are almost exclusively used by our party, and moist sugar is generally avoided. Dripping, too, is discontinued, and everything that is likely to whet the appetite is at a discount.

Drizzle-arich. — A Frenchman, soaked out of our bothy by the moisture of the weather, was overheard to exclaim "*Après moi le déluge.*"

Inverdreary.—Greatly to the indignation of their chief, several of the " Children of the Mist," in this romantic but rainy region, have assumed the garb of the Mackintoshes.

Loch Drunkie. — We have several partners in misery within hail, or life would be fairly washed out of us. We make up parties alternately at our

AMBIGUITY

Scene—*A Highland Ferry*

Tourist. "But we paid you sixpence each as we came over, and you said the same fare would bring us back."

Skipper. "Well, well, and I telled ye nothing but the truth, an' it'll be no more than the same fare I'm wantin' the noo for bringin' ye back."

shooting quarters when the weather allows of wading between them. Inebriation, it is to be feared, must be on the increase, for few of us who go out to dinner return without making a wet night of it.

Meantime, the watering-places in our vicinity— in particular the Linns o' Dun-Dreepie—are literally overflowing.

It is asserted that even young horses are growing impatient of the reins.

Our greatest comfort is the weekly budget of dry humour from *Mr. Punch.*

A DISAPPOINTING HOST.—*Sandy.* "A 'm tellt ye hev a new nebbur, Donal'." *Donald.* " Aye." *Sandy.* " An' what like is he ? " *Donald.* " Weel, he 's a curious laddie. A went to hev a bit talk wi' him th' ither evenin', an' he offered me a glass o' whuskey, d'ye see ? Weel, he was poorin' it oot, an' A said to him 'Stop ! '—*an' he stoppit !* That's the soort o' mon he is."

AUGUST IN SCOTLAND

Bag Carrier (to Keeper). " What does the maister aye ask that body tae shoot wi' him for? He canna hit a thing!"

Keeper. "Dod, man, I daur say he wishes they was a' like him. The same birds does him a' through the season!"

KINREEN O' THE DEE ;

A PIOBRACH HEARD WAILING DOWN GLENTANNER ON THE
EXILE OF THREE GENERATIONS.

Och hey, Kinreen o' the
Dee !
  Kinreen o' the Dee !
  Kinreen o' the Dee !
Och hey, Kinreen o' the
Dee !

I'll blaw up my chanter,
  I've rounded fu' weel,
To mony a ranter,
  In mony a reel,
An' pour'd a' my heart i' the
  win'bag wi' glee :
Och hey, Kinreen o' the
Dee !

For licht wis the laughter in bonny Kinreen,
An' licht wis the footfa' that glanced o'er the green,
An' licht ware the hearts a' an' lichtsome the eyne,
  Och hey, Kinreen o' the Dee !
    Kinreen o' the Dee !
    Kinreen o' the Dee !
  Och hey, Kinreen o' the Dee !

The auld hoose is bare noo,
  A cauld hoose to me,
The hearth is nae mair noo,
  The centre o' glee,

CANNY!

Sportsman. "That's a tough old fellow, Jemmy!"
Keeper. "Aye, sir, a grand bird to send to your freens!"

Mr. Punch in the Highlands

Nae mair for the bairnies the bield it has been,
Och hey, for bonny Kinreen!
The auld folk, the young folk, the wee anes, an' a',
A hunder years' hame birds are harried awa',
Are harried an' hameless, whatever winds blaw,
Och hey, Kinreen o' the Dee! &c.

Fareweel my auld pleugh lan',
I'll never mair pleugh it :
Fareweel my auld cairt an'
The auld yaud* that drew it.
Fareweel my auld kailyard, ilk bush an' ilk tree!
Och hey, Kinreen o' the Dee!
Fareweel the auld braes, that my hand keepit green,
Fareweel the auld ways where we waunder'd unseen
Ere the star o' my hearth came to bonny Kinreen,
Och hey, Kinreen o' the Dee! &c.

The auld kirk looks up o'er
The dreesome auld dead,
Like a saint speakin' hope o'er
Some sorrowfu' bed.
Fareweel the auld kirk, an' fareweel the kirk green,
They tell o' a far better hame than Kinreen!
The place we wad cling to—puir simple auld fules,
O' our births an' our bridals, oor blesses an' dools,
Whare oor wee bits o' bairnies lie cauld i' the mools,†
Och hey, Kinreen o' the Dee! &c.

I aft times hae wunder'd
If deer be as dear,
As sweet ties o' kindred,
To peasant or peer ;

* Mare.   † Earth.

80

EXPERTO CREDE

Tourist (*on approaching hostelry*). "What will you have, coachman?"

Driver. "A wee drap whuskey, sir, thank you."

Tourist. "All right. I'll get down and send it out to you."

Driver. "Na, na, gie me the saxpence. They'll gie you an unco sma' gless!"

As the tie to the hames o' the land born be,
    Och hey, Kinreen o' the Dee!
The heather that blossoms unkent o' the moor,
Wad dee in his lordship's best greenhoose, I'm sure,
To the wunder o' mony a fairy land flure.
        Och hey, Kinreen o' the Dee! &c.

    Though little the thing be,
        Oor ain we can ca';
    That little we cling be,
        The mair that it's sma';
Though puir wis oor hame, an' thogh wild wis the scene,
'Twas the hame o' oor hearts : it was bonnie Kinreen.
An yet we maun leave it, baith grey head an bairn ;
Leave it to fatten the deer o' Cock-Cairn,
O' Pannanich wuds, an' o' Morven o' Gairn.
        Och hey, Kinreen o' the Dee!
        Kinreen o' the Dee!
        Kinreen o' the Dee!
    Sae Fareweel for ever, Kinreen of the Dee!

A LAMENT FROM THE NORTH

"And then the weather's been so bad, Donald!"
"Ou ay, sir.   Only three fine days—and twa of them snappit up by the Sawbath!"

TWO ON A TOUR

" CAN you tell me which is Croft Lochay ? "

The smith leant on his pitchfork—he had been up at the hay—and eyed Gwendolen and myself with friendly interest.

" Ye'll be the gentry from London Mistress McDiarmat is expectin' ? "

" And which is the way to her house ? "

" Well," said the smith, shading his eyes as he peered up at the Ben, " ye can't see it rightly from here, as it lies behind yon knowe. It's a whole year whatever since I hev not been up myself; but if you follow the burn——"

I glanced at Gwen and saw that she shared my satisfaction. To cross the edge of civilisation had for months past been our hearts' desire ; and to have achieved a jumping-off place only approachable by a burn exceeded our wildest ambitions.

We thanked the smith, and set off on our expedition up the mountain side.

" We twa hae paidlit in the burn," sang Gwendolen as she skipped like a goat from stone to

ORIGIN OF THE HIGHLAND SCHOTTISCHE

"This is the way they tread the hay, tread the hay, tread the hay;
This is the way they tread the hay, tread the hay in Scotland!"

GROUSE SHOOTING LATE IN THE SEASON.
JOLLY, VERY!

"Come along, old fellow! Here's a point!!"

stone. "O Jack, isn't it too primitive and delightful!"

"Rather," said I, inhaling great draughts of the mountain air.

"Aren't you hungry?"

"Rather," I repeated. "Wonder what there'll be to eat."

"Oh, I don't care what it is. Anything will be delicious. Is that the house, do you think?"

I looked up and saw above us a low white-washed shanty covered with thatch which was kept in its place by a network of laths. A few heavy stones were evidently designed to keep the roof from blowing off in winter storms.

" No," said Gwen. " That must be the cowhouse byre, don't you call it ? "

" I'm not so sure," said I.

While we were still uncertain, a figure came to the door and bade us welcome.

DEER-STALKING MADE EASY. A HINT TO
LUSTY SPORTSMEN

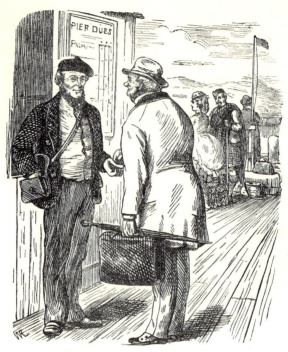

SOONER OR LATER

Old Gent. "When is the steamer due here?"
Highland Pier-Master. "Various. Sometimes sooner, sometimes earlier, an' even sometimes before that, too."

"HARMLESS"

Cockney Sporting Gent. "But I think it's a 'en!"
Sandy (*his keeper*). "Shŏot, man, shŏot! She'll be no muckle the waur o' ye!!"

"Come in, come in. Ye'll be tired with the travelling, and ye'll like to see the rooms."

We acquiesced, and Mistress McDiarmat led the way into the cow-house.

"Shoo!" she cried as she opened the door of the bedroom. "Get away, Speckle! The hens *will* lay their bit egg on the bed, sir."

"What fresh eggs we shall get!" cried Gwen, delighted with this fresh proof of rusticity and with the Gaelic gutturals with which Mistress McDiarmat emphasized her remarks to Speckle.

The "other end" was furnished with two hard chairs, a table and a bed.

"Fancy a bed in the dining-room and hens in your bed!" said Gwen, in the highest of spirits. "And here comes tea! Eggs and bacon—Ah! how lovely they smell, and how much nicer than horrid, stodgy dinners! And oatcakes—and jelly —and the lightest feathery scones! O Jack, isn't it heavenly?"

"Rather," I agreed, beginning the meal with tremendous gusto. The eggs and bacon disappeared in the twinkling of an eye, and then we fell to on the light feathery scones. "Wish we

PLEASANT

Friend (to novice at salmon fishing). "I say, old boy, mind how you wade; there are some tremendous holes, fourteen or fifteen feet deep."

hadn't wasted a fortnight's time and money in ruinous Highland hotels. Wonder what Schiehallion thinks of hot baths and late dinners, not to speak of waiters and wine-lists."

"I suppose," remarked Gwendolen, "one *could* get a bath at the Temperance Inn we passed on the road?"

"Baths!" cried I. "Why, my dear, one only has to go and sit under the neighbouring waterfall."

Gwen did not laugh, and looking up I saw she

AN IMPORTANT DETAIL

Our latest Millionaire (to Gillie, who has brought him within close range of the finest stag in the forest). "I say, Mac, confound it all, *which eye do you use?*"

92

English Tourist (*in the far North, miles from anywhere*).
" Do you mean to say that you and your family live here
all the winter ?   Why, what do you do when any of you
are ill ?   You can never get a doctor ! "
Scotch Shepherd.   " Nae, sir.   We've just to dee a natural
death ! "

had stopped in the middle of a scone on which she
had embarked with great appetite.

" Try an oat-cake," I suggested.

" No, thanks," said Gwen.

" A little more jelly ? "

Gwen shook her head.

I finished my meal in silence and pulled out my
pipe.

SCENE—A ROADSIDE INN IN A MOORLAND DISTRICT, SCOTLAND

(The Captain and Gamekeeper call in to have some Refreshment)

Landlady (enters in fear). " Eh, sir, yer gun's no loaded is't ? for a never would bide in a hoose whaur the wur a loaded gun in a' m'life."

Captain (composedly). " Oh, we'll soon put that all right —have you got a cork ? "

    [*Exit Landlady and brings a cork, which the Captain carefully sticks in the muzzle of the gun, and assures her it is all right now—*

Landlady (relieved). " Ou, aye ! it's a' right noo, but it wasna safe afore, ye ken."

" Going to smoke in here ? " asked Gwen.

" It's raining outside, my dear."

" Oh, very well. But remember this is my bed-room. I decline to sleep with hens."

I put the pipe away and prepared for conversation.

94

"A MONARCH OF THE GLEN"

Transatlantic Millionaire (surveying one of his deer-forests). "Ha! look there! I see *three excursionists!* Send 'em to the —— !"

Gigantic Gillie (and chucker-out). "If you please, Mr. Dollers, they're *excisemen!*"

T. M. "I don't care *who* they are! Send 'em to the —— !"

G. G. "Yes, Mr. Dollers." [*Proceeds to carry out order.*

Sportsman (who declines to be told where to go and what to do by his gillie), after an arduous stalk in the blazing sun, at last manages to crawl within close range of those "brown specks" he discovered miles distant on the hill-side!

"Can't you sit still?" asked Gwen after a long pause.

"This chair is very hard, dear."

"So is mine."

"Don't you think we might sit on the bed?"

"Certainly not. I shouldn't sleep a wink if we disarranged the clothes, and only an expert can re-make a chaff bed."

"Wish we had something to read," I remarked, after another long pause.

PROMISING!

Tourist. " Have you any decent cigars ? "

Highland Grocer. " Decent cigars ? Ay, here are decent cigars enough."

Tourist. " Are they Havanahs, or Manillas ? "

Highland Grocer. " They're just from Kircaldy ! "

" Do you expect a circulating library on the top of Ben-y-Gloe ? "

I began to realise that Gwen was no longer in a conversational mood, and made no further efforts to break the silence. Half-an-hour later Gwen came across the room and laid her hand on my shoulder. " What are you reading, dear ? " she asked.

" I find we can get a train from Struan to-morrow afternoon which catches the London connection at Perth when the train's not more than two hours late."

" We can't risk that. Isn't there a train in the morning ? "

" It would mean leaving this at five."

" So much the better. O Jack, if I eat another meal like that it will be fatal. To think we shall be back in dear old Chelsea to-morrow ! "

"THE MISS"

Gillie. "Eh, mon! But it's fortunate there's beef in Aberdeen!"

G 2

MR. BRIGGS IN THE HIGHLANDS

By JOHN LEECH

Mr. Briggs, feeling that his heart is in the Highlands
a-chasing the deer, starts for the North.

Before going out, Mr. Briggs and his friends have a quiet chat about deer-stalking generally. He listens with much interest to some pleasing anecdotes about the little incidents frequently met with—such as balls going through caps—toes being shot off!—occasionally being gored by the antlers of infuriate stags, &c., &c., &c.

Mr. Briggs, previous to going through his course of deer-stalking, assists the forester in getting a hart or two for the house. Donald is requesting our friend to hold the animal down by the horns.

[N.B. The said animal is as strong as a bull, and uses his legs like a race-horse.

The deer are driven for Mr. Briggs. He has an excellent place, but what with waiting by himself so long, the murmur of the stream, the beauty of the scene, and the novelty of the situation, he falls asleep, and while he takes his forty winks, the deer pass!

As the wind is favourable, the deer are driven again.

Mr. Briggs is suddenly face to face with the monarch of the glen! He is so astonished that he omits to fire his rifle.

To-day he goes out for a stalk, and Donald shows Mr. Briggs
the way!

After a good deal of climbing, our friend gets to the top of Ben-
something-or-other, and the forester looks out to see if there are any
deer on the hills. Yes! several hinds, and perhaps the finest hart
that ever was seen

To get at him, they are obliged to go a long way round. Before they get down, the shower, peculiar to the country, overtakes them, so they "shelter a-wee."

With extraordinary perseverance they come within shot of "the finest hart." Mr. B. is out of breath, afraid of slipping, and wants to blow his nose (quite out of the question), otherwise he is tolerably comfortable.

After aiming for a quarter of an hour, Mr. B. fires both his barrels—and— misses!!!! *Tableau*—The forester's anguish

The royal hart Mr. Briggs did NOT hit.

Mr. Briggs has another day's stalking, and his rifle having gone off sooner than he expected, he kills a stag. As it is his first, he is made free of the forest by the process customary on the hills!—

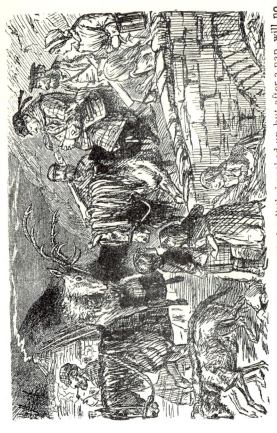

And returns home in triumph. He is a little knocked up, but after a nap, will, no doubt, go through the broad-sword dance in the evening as usual.

MR. BRIGGS GROUSE SHOOTING

9 A.M. His arrival on the moor.—Mr. Briggs says that the fine bracing air makes him so vigorous that he shall never be beat. He also facetiously remarks that he is on "his native heath," and that his "name is Macgregor!"

[The result of the day's sport will be communicated by electric telegraph.

SKETCHES FROM SCOTLAND

AT THE DRUMQUHIDDER HIGHLAND GATHERING.

SCENE—*A meadow near Drumquhidder, South Perthshire, where the annual Highland Games are being held. The programme being a long one, there are generally three events being contested in various parts of the ground at the same time. On the benches immediately below the Grand Stand are seated two Drumquhidder worthies,* MR. PARRITCH *and* MR. HAVERS, *with* MRS. MCTAVISH *and her niece, two acquaintances from Glasgow, to whom they are endeavouring — not altogether successfully—to make themselves agreeable.*

Mr. Havers (*in allusion to the dozen or so of drags, landaus, and waggonettes on the ground*). There's a number o' machines hier the day, Messis McTarvish, an' a wonderfu' crood ; there'll be a bit scarceness ower on yon side, but a gey many a'thegither. I conseeder we're jest awfu' forrtunate in the day an' a'.

"MISTAKEN IDENTITY"

SCENE—*Northern Meeting at Inverness.* PERSONS REPRE-
SENTED—Ian Gorm *and* Dougald Mohr, *gillies.* Mr.
Smith, *of London.*

First Gillie. "Wull yon be the MacWhannel, Ian
Gorm?"

Second ditto. "No!! Hes nae-um is Muster Smuth!
And he ahl-ways wears the kult—and it is foohl that you
aar, Tougalt Mohr!!"

[*Mrs. McTavish assents, but without enthusiasm.*

Mr. Parritch. I've jist ben keekin into the
Refraishmen' Tent. It's an awfu' peety they're no
pairmeetin' ony intoaxicans—naethin' but non-
alcohoalic liquors an' sic like, an' the hawm-sawnd-
wiches no verra tender. (*With gallantry.*) What
do ye say, noo, Messis McTarvish—wull ye **no**
come an' tak' a bite wi' me?

Mrs. McTavish (*distantly*). Ah'm no feelin' able for't jist the noo, Mester Pairritch.

Mr. Parr. Ye'll hae a boatle o' leemonade at my expense ? Ye'll no ? Then ye wull, Mess Rawse. (*With relief, as Miss Rose declines also.*) Aweel, I jist thocht I'd pit the quaistion. (*To a friend of his, who joins them.*) An' hoo's a' wi' ye, Mester McKerrow ? Ye're a member o' the Cawmittee, I obsairve, sae I'll hae to keck up a bet row wi' ye.

Mr. McKerrow (*unconcernedly*). Then ye'll jist to hae to keck it doon again. What's wrang the noo ?

Mr. Parr. I'd like to ask ye if ye conseeder it fair or jest to charrge us tippence every time we'd gc aff the groon ? Man, it's jist an extoartion.

Mr. McKerr. I'm no responsible for 't ; but, if *I*'d ben there, I'd ha' chairged ye twa shellins ; sae ye'd better say nae mair aboot the maitter.

[*Mr. Parritch does not pursue the subject.*

Mr. Havers (*as a detachment of the Black Watch Highlanders conclude an exhibition of musical drill*). Ye'll be the baiter o' haeing the Block Wetch hier the day Man, they gie us a colour ! It's verra

(LOCH) FYNE GRAMMAR

(*A Sad Fact for the School Board*)

Tugal. 'Dud ye'll ever see the *I-oo-na* any more before?"

Tonal. " Surely I was."

Tugal. " Ay, ay! Maybe you was never on poard too, after thus——"

Tonal. " I dud."

pretty hoo nicely they can pairforrm the drill. . . . An' noo them sojers is gaun to rin a bet race amang theirsels. This 'll be an extry cawmpetee-tion, I doot. (*As the race is being run.*) It's no a verra suitable dress for rinnin'—the spleughan—or "sporran," is it?—hairrts them tairible.

Mr. McKerr. (*contradictiously*). The sporran does na hairrt them at a'.

Mr. Havers. Man, it's knockin' against them at every stride they tak'. (*His attention wanders to a Highland Fling, which three small boys are dancing on a platform opposite.*) He's an awfu' bonnie dauncer that wee laddie i' the meddle!

Mr. McKerr. Na sae awfu' bonnie, he luiks tae much at his taes. Yon on the richt is the laddie o' the lote! he disna move his boady at a'. . . . This'll be the Half Mile Handicap they're stairting for down yonder. It'll gae to Jock Alister—him in the blue breeks.

Mr. Parr. Yon grup-luikin' tyke? I canna thenk it.

Mr. Havers. Na, it'll be yon bald-heided man in broon. He's verra enthusiastic. He's ben rinnin' in a' the races, I obsairve. "Smeth" did

NON BEN (LOMOND) TROVATO.

Rory (fresh from the hills). "Hech, mon! Ye're loassin' a' yer watter!!"

Aungus. "Haud yer tongue, ye feul! Ett's latt oot to stoap the laddies frae ridin' ahint!!"

117

ye say his neem was ? (*To Miss Rose, "pawkily."*)
Ye'll hae an affaictionate regaird for that neem, I'm
thenking, Mess Rawse ?

Miss Rose (*with maidenly displeasure*). 'Deed,
an I'm no unnerstanding why ye should thenk ony
sic a thing !

Mr. Havers (*abashed*). I beg your pairrdon. I
don't know hoo it was I gethered Smeth was your
ain neem. (*Miss Rose shakes her head.*) No ?
Then maybe ye'll be acquaint with a Mester Alex-
awnder Smeth fro' Paisley ? (*Miss Rose is not,
nor apparently desires to be, and Mr. Havers returns
to the foot-race.*) The baldheid's leadin' them a', I
tellt ye he'd—— Na, he's gien up ! it'll be the little
block fellow, he's peckin' up tairible !

Mr. Parr. 'Twull no be him. Yon lang chap
has an easy jobe o't. Ye'll see he'll jist putt a
spairrt on at yon faur poast—he's comin' on noo—
he's . . . Losh ! he's only thirrd after a'; he
didna putt the spairrt on sune eneugh ; that was
the gran' fau't he made !

Mr. Havers. They'll be begenning the wrustling
oot yon in the centre. . . . (*As the competitors
grip.*) Losh ! that's no the way to wrustle ; they

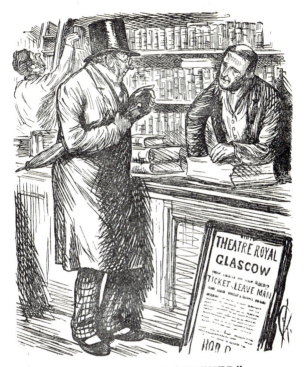

"NOTHING LIKE LEATHER"

Bookseller (to Lanarkshire country gentleman who had brought his back numbers to be bound). "Would you like them done in 'Russia' or 'Morocco,' sir?"

Old Gentleman. "Na, never maind aboot Rooshy or Moroccy. I'll just hae 'em boond in Glasgy here!"

"That's jist the game, I'm telling ye; ye know naething at
a' aboot it!"

shouldna left the ither up ; they're no allowed to
threp!

Mr. McKerr. That's jist the game, I'm telling
ye ; ye know naething at a' aboot it!

Mr. Havers. I'd sthruggle baiter'n that mysel',
it's no great wrustling at a', merely bairrns'
play!

Mr. McKerr. (as a corpulent elderly gentleman

THE TROUBLES OF STALKING

Irate Gillie (on discovering in the distance, for the third time that morning, a " brute of a man " moving about in his favourite bit of "forest "). " Oh! deil take the people! Come awa', Muster Brown, sir ; *it's just Peekadilly ! ! !*"

appears, in very pink tights). Ye'll see some science noo, for hier's McBannock o' Balwhuskie, the chawmpion.

Mr. Havers (*disenchanted*). Wull yon be him in the penk breeks. Man, but he's awfu' stoot for sic wark !

Mr. McKerr. The wecht of him's no easy put doon. The rest are boys to him.

Mr. Parr. I doot the little dairk fellow'll hae him . . . it's a gey sthruggle.

Mr. McKerr. He's not doon yet. Wull ye bait sexpence against McBannock, Mester Pairritch ?

Mr. Parr. (*promptly*). Aye, wull I—na, he's got the dairk mon doon. I was jist mindin' the sword-daunce, sae the bait's aff. (*Three men in full Highland costume step upon the platform and stand, proud and impassive, fronting the grand stand, while the judges walk round them, making careful notes of their respective points.*) What wull *they* be aboot ?

Mr. McKerr. It'll be the prize for the mon who's the best dressed Hielander at his ain expense. I'm thenkin' they'll find it no verra easy to come to a deceesion.

A FALLEN ASS

Indignant Gillie (to Jones, of London, who has by mistake killed a hind). "I thoucht ony fule ken't it was the stags that had the horns!"

BONCHIENIE

Young Lady Tourist (caressing the hotel terrier, Bareglourie, N.B.). "Oh, Binkie is his name! He seems inclined to be quite friendly with me."

Waiter. "Oo, aye, miss, he's no vera parteec'lar wha he taks oop wi!"

Mr. Parr. Deed, it's no sae deeficult ; 'twill be the mon in the centre, sure as deith !

Mr. Havers. Ye say that because he has a' them gowd maidles hing on his jocket !

Mr. Parr. (loftily). I pay no attention to the maidles at a'. I'm sayin' that Dougal Macrae is the best dressed Hielander o' the three.

Mr. Havers. It'll no be Macrae at a'. Jock McEwan, that's furthest west, 'll be the mon.

Mr. Parr. (dogmatically). It'll be Macrae, I'm

tellin' ye. He has the nicest kelt on him that iver I sa'!

Mr. Havers. It's no the *kelt* that diz it, 'tis jist the way they pit it on. An' Macrae'll hae his tae faur doon, a guid twa enches too low, it is.

Mr. Parr. Ye're a' wrang, the kelt is on richt eneugh!

"CANNY"

First North Briton. "'T's a fine day, this?"
Second ditto. "No ill, ava."
First ditto. "Ye'll be travellin'?"
Second ditto. "Weel, maybe I'm no."
First ditto. "Gaun t'Aberdeen, maybe?"
Second ditto. "Ye're no faur aff't!!"
　　　　[*Mutually satisfied, each goes his respective way*

Mr. Havers. I know fine hoo a kelt should be pit an, though I'm no Hielander mysel', and I'll ask ye, Mess Rawse, if Dougal Macrae's kelt isn't too lang ; it's jist losin his knees a' thegither, like a lassie he looks in it !

[*Miss Rose declines, with some stiffness, to express an opinion on so delicate a point.*

Mr. Parr. (recklessly). I'll pit a sexpence on Macrae wi' ye, come noo !

Mr. Havers. Na, na, pit cawmpetent jedges on to deceede, and they'll be o' my opeenion ; but I'll no bait wi' ye.

Mr. Parr. (his blood up). Then I'll hae a sexpence on 't wi *you*, Mester McKerrow !

Mr. McKerr. Nay, I'm for Macrae mysel' . . . An' we're baith in the richt o't too, for they've jist gien him the bit red flag—that means he's got firsst prize.

Mr. Parr. (to Mr. Havers, with reproach). Man, if ye'd hed the speerit o' your opeenions, I'd ha' won sexpence aff ye by noo !

Mr. Havers (obstinately). I canna thenk but that Macrae's kelt was too lang—prize or no prize.

THE PURCHASING LIMIT

Mr. Steinsen (our latest millionaire—after his third fruitless stalk). "Now, look here, you rascal! if you can't have the brutes tamer, I'm hanged if I don't sack you!"

I'll be telling him when I see him that he looked like a lassie in it.

Mr. Parr. (*with concern*). I wouldna jist advise ye to say ony sic a thing to him. These Hie-landers are awfu' prood ; and he micht tak' it gey ill fro' ye !

Mr. Havers. I see nae hairrm mysel' in jist tellin' him, in a pleesant, daffin-like way, that he looked like a lassie in his kelt. But there's nae tellin' hoo ye may offend some fowk ; an' I'm thenking it's no sae verra prawbable that I'll hae the oaportunity o' saying onything aboot the maitter to him.

AWKWARD FOR HIM.—*Tam.* " I'm sayin', man, my cairt o' hay's fa'en ower. Will ye gie 's a haund up wi' 't ? " *Jock.* " 'Deed will I. But ye'll be in nae hurry till I get tae the end o' the raw ? " *Tam.* " Ou no. I'm in nae hurry, but I doot my faither 'll be wearyin'." *Jock.* " An' whaur's yer faither ? " *Tam.* " He's in below the hay ! "

GROWING POPULARITY OF THE HIGHLANDS

Mrs. Smith (of Brixton). "Lor', Mr. Brown, I 'ardly knoo yer! Only think of our meetin' *'ere*, this year, instead of dear old Margit! An' I suppose that's the costume you go *salmon-stalking* in?"

MORE SKETCHES FROM SCOTLAND

On a Callander Char-a-banc.

Scene—*In front of the Trossachs Hotel. The few passengers bound for Callander have been sitting for several minutes on the coach "Fitz-James" in pelting rain, resignedly wondering when the driver will consider them sufficiently wet to start.*

The Head Boots (to the driver). There's another to come yet; he'll no be lang now. (*The cause of the delay comes down the hotel steps, and surveys the vehicle and its occupants with a surly scowl.*) Up with ye, sir, plenty of room on the second seats.

The Surly Passenger. And have all the umbrellas behind dripping on my hat! No, thank you, I'm going in front. (*He mounts, and takes up the apron.*) Here, driver, just look at this apron— it's sopping wet!

The Driver (tranquilly). Aye, I'm thinking it wull ha' got a bet domp.

130

"Ou aye, ye can get inside the boot if ye've a mind to it."

The Surly P. Well, I'm not going to have this over *me.* Haven't you got a *dry* one some-where?

The Driver. There'll be dry ones at Collander.

The Surly P. (*with a snort*). At Callander! Much good that is! (*With crushing sarcasm.*) If I'm to keep dry on this concern, it strikes me I'd better get inside the boot at once!

The Driver (*with the air of a man who is making a concession*). Ou aye, ye can get inside the boot if ye've a mind to it.

[*The coach starts, and is presently stopped at a corner to take up a male and a female passenger, who occupy the seats immediately behind the Surly Passenger.*

The Female P. (*enthusiastically, to her companion*). There's dear old Mrs. Macfarlane, come out to see the last of us! Look at her standing out there in the garden, all in the rain. That's what I always *say* about the Scotch—they *are* warm-hearted!

[*She waves her hand in farewell to some distant object.*

Her Companion. That ain't her; that's an old

"MEN WERE DECEIVERS EVER"

Mr. Punch is at present in the Highlands "a-chasing the deer."

Mrs. Punch is at home, and has promised all her friends haunches of venison as soon as they arrive!

apple-tree in the garden *you*'re waving to. *She*'s keeping indoors—and shows her sense too.

The Female P. (disgusted). Well, I *do* think after our being at the farm a fortnight and all, she *might——* But that's Scotch all *over*, that is ; get all they *can* out of you, and then, for anything *they* care——!

"DESIRABLE"

Saxon Passenger (on Highland coach). "Of course you're well acquainted with the country round about here. Do you know ' Glen Accron ' ? "

Driver. "Aye, weel."

Saxon Passenger (who had just bought the estate). "What sort of a place is it ? "

Driver. "Weel, if ye saw the deil tethered on't, ye'd just say ' Puir brute ' ! "

ISOLATION!—OFF THE ORKNEYS

Southern Tourist. "'Get any newspapers here?"

Orcadian Boatman. "Ou aye, when the steamer comes. If it's fine, she'll come ance a week; but when it's stormy, i' winter, we dinna catch a glint o' her for three months at a time."

S. T. "Then you'll not know what's goin' on in London!"

O. B. "Na—but ye see ye're just as ill aff i' London as we are, for ye dinna ken what's gaun on here!"

The Surly P. I don't know whether you are aware of it, ma'am, but that umbrella of yours is sending a constant trickle down the back of my neck, which is *most* unpleasant!

The Female P. I'm sorry to hear it, sir, but it's no worse for you than it is for me. I've got somebody else's umbrella dripping down *my* back, and *I* don't complain.

The Surly P. I *do*, ma'am, for, being in front, I haven't even the poor consolation of feeling that my umbrella is a nuisance to anybody.

A Sardonic P. (*in the rear, politely*). On the contrary, sir, I find it a most pleasing object to contemplate. Far more picturesque, I don't doubt, than any scenery it may happen to conceal.

A Chatty P. (*to the driver; not because he cares, but simply for the sake of conversation*). What fish do you catch in that river there?

The Driver (*with an effort*). There'll be troots, an', maybe, a pairrch or two.

The Chatty P. Perch? Ah, that's rather like a goldfish in shape, eh?

Driver (*cautiously*). Aye, it would be that.

Chatty P. Only considerably bigger, of course.

Driver (*evasively*). Pairrch is no a verra beg fesh.

Chatty P. But bigger than goldfish.

Driver (*more confidently*). Ou aye, they'll be begger than goldfesh.

Chatty P. (*persistently*). You've seen goldfish— know what they're *like*, eh?

Driver (*placidly*). I canna say I do.

[*They pass a shooting party with beaters.*

ON THE MOORS

The Laird's Brother-in-law (from London). "It's very strange, Lachlan! I'm having no luck!—and yet I seem to see two birds in place of one? That was surely very strong whiskey your master gave me at lunch?"

Keeper. "Maybe aye and maybe no—the whuskey was goot; but any way ye dinna manage to hit the richt bird o' the twa'!"

Chatty P. (*as before*).   What are they going to shoot ?

Driver.   They'll jist be going up to the hells foɪ a bet grouse drivin'.

A Lady P.   I wonder why they carry those poles with the red and yellow flags.   I suppose they're to warn tourists to keep out of range when they begin firing at the butts.   I know they *have* butts up on the moor, because I've seen them. Just look at those birds running after that man throwing grain for them.   Would those be *grouse ?*

Driver.   Ye'll no find grouse so tame as that, mem ;   they'll jist be phaysants.

The Lady P.   Poor dear things !   why, they're as tame as chickens.   It *does* seem so cruel to kill them !

Her Comp.   Well, but   they   kill   chickens, occasionally.

The Lady P.   Not with a horrid gun ;   and, besides, that's such a totally different thing.

The Chatty P.   What do you call that mountain, driver, eh ?

Driver.   Yon hell?   I'm no minding its name.

The Surly P.   You don't seem very ready in

A POOR ADVERTISEMENT

Tourist. "I suppose you feel proud to have such a distinguished man staying in your house?"

Host of the "Drumdonnachie Arms." "'Deed no! A body like that does us mair hairm than guid; his appearance is nae credit tae oor commissariat!"

GENEROSITY

Noble Lord (whose rifle has brought to a scarcely untimely end a very consumptive-looking fallow deer). " Tut—t, t, t, t, tut! O, I say, Stubbs!"—*(to his keeper)*—"you shouldn't have let me kill such a poor, little, sickly, scraggy thing as this, you know! It positively isn't fit for human food! Ah! look here, now! I'll tell you what. You and McFarlin may have this buck between you!!!"

pointing out the objects of interests on the route, I must say.

Driver (modestly). There'll be them on the corch that know as much aboot it as myself. *(After a pause—to vindicate his character as a cicerone.)* Did ye nottice a bit building at the end of the loch over yonder ?

The Surly P. No, I didn't.

Driver. Ye might ha' seen it, had ye looked.

[*He relapses into a contented silence.*

TRAVELLER TOO BONÂ FIDE

Dusty Pedestrian. "I should like a glass of beer, missis, please——"

Landlady. "Hae ye been trevellin' by rell?"

Pedestrian. "No, I've been walking—fourteen miles."

Landlady. "Na, na, nae drink will ony yin get here, wha's been pleesure-seekin' o' the Sawbath day!!"

141

Chatty P. Anything remarkable about the building ?

Driver. It was no the building that's remairkable. (*After a severe struggle with his own reticence.*) It was jist the spoat. 'Twas there *Roderick Dhu* fought *Fitz-James* after convoying him that far on his way.

[*The Surly Passenger snorts as though he didn't consider this information.*

The Lady P. (*who doesn't seem to be up in her* " *Lady of the Lake* "). *Fitz-James who ?*

Her Comp. I fancy he's the man who owns this line of coaches. There's his name on the side of this one.

The Lady P. And I saw *Roderick Dhu's* on another coach. I *thought* it sounded familiar, somehow. He must be the *rival* proprietor, I suppose. I wonder if they've made it up yet.

The Driver (*to the Surly Passenger, with another outburst of communicativeness*). Yon stoan is called " Sawmson's Putting Stoan." He hurrled it up to the tope of the hell, whaur it's bided ever sence.

[*The Surly Passenger receives this information with an incredulous grunt.*

142

MR. PUNCH IN THE HIGHLANDS

He goes on board the *Iona*. The only drawback to his perfect enjoyment is the jealousy caused among all the gentlemen by the ladies clustering round him on all occasions.

The Lady P. What a magnificent old ruin that is across the valley, some ancient castle, evidently ; they can't build like that nowadays !

The Driver. That's the Collander Hydro-pawthec, mem ; burrnt doon two or three years back.

The Lady P. (*with a sense of the irony of events*). *Burnt* down ! A Hydropathic ! Fancy !

Male P. (*as they enter Callander and pass a trim villa*). There, *that's* Mr. Figgis's place.

His Comp. What—*that ?* Why, it's quite a *bee-yutiful* place, with green venetians, and a conservatory, and a croaky lawn, and everything ! Fancy all that belonging to *him !* It's well to be a grocer—in *these* parts, seemingly !

Male P. Ah, *we* ought to come up and start business here ; it 'ud be better than being in the Caledonian Road !

> [*They meditate for the remainder of the journey upon the caprices of Fortune with regard to grocery profits in Caledonia and the Caledonian Road respectively.*

PREHISTORIC PEEPS

There were often unforeseen circumstances which gave to the Highland stalking of those days an added zest!

THE PLEASURES OF TRAVEL

(By Ane that has kent them)

'Tis a great thing, the Traivel; I'll thank
    ye tae find
Its equal for openin' the poors o' the mind.
It mak's a man polished, an' gies him, ye
    ken,
Sic a graun' cosmypollitan knowledge o'
    men !

I ne'er was a stay-at-hame callant ava.
I aye must be rantin' an' roamin' awa',
An' far hae I wandered, an' muckle hae seen
O' the ways o' the warl' wi' ma vara ain een.

I've been tae Kingskettle wi' Wullie an' Jeames,
I've veesited Anster an' Elie an' Wemyss,
I've walked tae Kirkca'dy an' Cupar an' Crail,
An' I aince was awa' tae Dundee wi' the rail.

Losh me, sir ! The wonnerfu' things that I saw !
The kirks wi' their steeples, sae bonny an' braw,
An' publics whauriver ye turned wi' yer ee—
'Tis jist a complete eddication, Dundee !

Theer's streets—be the hunner ! An' shops be the score !
Theer's bakers an' grocers an' fleshers galore !
An' milliners' winders a' flauntin' awa'
Wi' the last o' the fashions frae Lunnon an' a'.

146

"WINGED"

First Gael. "What's the matter, Tonal?"
Second ditto (who had been out with Old Briggs). "Matter! Hur legs is full o' shoots"

An' eh, sic a thrang, sir !   I saw in a minnit
Mair folk than the toun o' Kinghorn will hae in it
I wadna hae thocht that the hail o' creation
Could boast at ae time sic a vast population !

Ma word, sir !   It gars ye clap haun' tae yer broo
An' wunner what's Providence after the noo
That he lets sic a swarm o' they cratur's be born
Wham naebody kens aboot here in Kinghorn.

What ?—Leeberal minded?—Ye canna but be
When ye've had sic a graun' eddication as me.
For oh, theer is naethin' like traivel, ye ken,
For growin' acquent wi' the natur' o' men.

———

" FALLS OF FOYERS."—A correspondent writes :
—" I have seen a good many letters in the *Times*,
headed ' The Falls of the Foyers.'   Here and abroad
I have seen many Foyers, and only fell down once.
This was at the Théâtre Francais, where the Foyer
is kept highly polished, or used to be so.   If the
Foyers are carpeted or matted, there need be no
' Falls.'   Yours,   COMMON SENSE."

MR. PUNCH AT THE HIGHLAND GAMES

Shows the natives how to "put the stone."

AN ARTIST SCAMP IN THE HIGHLANDS

Artist (entering). "My good woman, if you'll allow me, I'll just paint that bedstead of yours."

Cottager (with bob-curtsey). "Thank ye, sir, I' sure it's very kind of ye—but dinna ye think that little one over yonder wants it more?"

EN ÉCOSSE

À Monsieur Punch

DEAR MISTER,—I come of to make a little voyage in Scotland. Ah, the beautiful country of Sir Scott, Sir Wallace, and Sir Burns! I am gone to render visit to one of my english friends, a

ZEAL

Saxon Tourist. "Been at the kirk?"

Celt. "Aye."

Saxon T. "How far is it?"

Celt. "Daur say it'll be fourteen mile."

Saxon T. "Fourteen miles!!"

Celt. "Aye, aw'm awfu' fond o' the preachin'"

charming boy—*un charmant garçon*—and his wife, a lady very instructed and very spiritual, and their childs. I adore them, the dear little english childs, who have the cheeks like some roses, and the hairs like some flax, as one says in your country, all buckled—*bouclés*, how say you ?

I go by the train of night—in french one says "*le sleeping*"—to Edimbourg, and then to Calendar, where I attend to find a coach—in french one says "*un mail*" or "*un fourinhand.*" *Nom d'une pipe*, it is one of those ridicule carriages, called in french "*un breack*," and in english a char-à-banc—that which the english pronounce "*tcherribaingue*"— which attends us at the going out of the station ! Eh well, in voyage one must habituate himself to all ! But a such carriage discovered—*découverte*— seems to me well unuseful in a country where he falls of rain without cease.

Before to start I demand of all the world some *renseignements* on the scottish climate, and all the world responds me, "All-days of the rain." By consequence I procure myself some impermeable vestments, one mackintosch coat, one mackintosch cape of Inverness, one mackintosch covering of

152

THRIFT

Peebles Body (to townsman who was supposed to be in London on a visit). "E—eh Mac! ye're sune hame again!"

Mac. "E—eh, it's just a ruinous place, that! Mun, a had na' been the-erre abune twa hoours when—*bang*—went s.ixpence!!!"

voyage, one south-western hat, some umbrellas, some gaiters, and many pairs of boots very thick— not boots of town, but veritable "shootings."

I arrive at Edimbourg by a morning of the most

A SATISFACTORY SOLUTION

"I fear, Duncan, that friend of mine does not seem overly safe with his gun."

"No, sir. But I'm thinkin' it'll be all right if you wass to go wan side o' him and Mr. John the ither. He canna shoot baith o' ye!"

"VITA FUMUS"

Tonal. "Whar'll ye hae been till, Tugal?"
Tugal. "At ta McTavishes' funeral——"
Tonal. "An' is ta Tavish deed?"
Tugal. "Deed is he!!"
Tonal. "Losh, mon! Fowk are aye deein' noo that never used to dee afore!!"

PRECAUTIONS

Saxon Angler (to his keeper). " You seem in a great hurry with your clip! I haven't seen a sign of a fish yet—not a rise ! "

Duncan. " 'Deed, sir, I wisna a botherin' mysel' aboot the fush ; but seein' you wis new to the business, I had a thocht it widna be lang afore you were needin' a left oot o' the watter yoursel' ! "

sads ; the sky grey, the earth wet, the air humid. Therefore I propose to myself to search at Calender a place at the interior, *et voilà*—and see there— the *breack* has no interior ! There is but that which one calls a "boot," and me, Auguste, can I to lie myself there at the middle of the baggages ? Ah no ! Thus I am forced to endorse—*endosser*—my impermeable vestments and to protect myself the

HIS POUND OF FLESH

Financier (*tenant of our forest, after a week's unsuccessful stalking*). "Now, look here, my man. I bought and paid for ten stags. If the brutes can't be shot, you'll have to trap them! I've promised the venison, and I mean to have it!"

head by my south-western hat. Then, holding firmly the most strong of my umbrellas, I say to the coacher, "He goes to fall of the rain, is it not?" He makes a sign of head of not to comprehend. Ah, for sure, he is scottish! I indicate the sky and my umbrella, and I say "Rain?" and then he comprehends. "*Eh huile,*" he responds to me, "*ah canna sé, mébi huile no hé meukl the dé.*" I write this phonetically, for I comprehend not the scottish language. What droll of conversation! Him comprehends not the english; me I comprehend not the scottish.

But I essay of new, "How many has he of it from here to the lake? *C'est inutile*—it is unuseful. I say, "Distance?" He comprehends. "*Mébi oui taque toua hours,*" says he; "*beutt yile no fache yoursel, its no sé lang that yile bi ouishinn yoursel aoua.*" *Quelle langue*—what language, even to write phonetically! I comprehend one sole word, "hours." Some hours! *Sapristi!* I say, "Hours?" He says "*Toua*" all together, a monosyllable. *Sans aucune doute ça veut dire* "twelve"—*douze.* Twelve hours on a *breack* in a such climate! Ah, no! *C'est trop fort*—it is

SCRUPULOUS

Shepherd. "O, Jims, mun! Can ye no gie a whustle on tha ram'lin' brute o' mine? I daurna mysel'; it's just fast-day in oor parish!!"

too strong! "Hold," I cry myself, "attend, I descend, I go not!" It is true that I see not how I can to descend, for I am *entouré*—how say you? of voyagers. We are five on a bench, of the most narrows, and me I am at the middle. And the bench before us is also complete, and we touch him of the knees. And my neighbours carry on the knees all sorts of packets, umbrellas, canes, sacks of voyage, &c. *Il n'y a pas moyen*—he has not there mean. And the coacher says me "*Na, na, monne, yile no ghitt doun, yile djest baïd ouar yer sittinn.*" Then he mounts to his place, and we part immediately. *Il va tomber de la pluie! Douze heures! Mon Dieu, quel voyage!*

Agree, &c.,

AUGUSTE.

"THE LAND OF LORN"

*It has drizzled incessantly, for a fortnight, since the Smiths came down to
their charming villa at Braebogie, in Argyleshire.*

*Keeper (who has come up to say the boat is ready on the loch, if "they're for fushin' the
day").* "Eh! I should na wonder if this weather tur-rns ta rain!!"

EN ÉCOSSE (ENCORE)

À Monsieur Punch

DEAR MISTER,—I have spoken you of my departure from Calendar on the *breack*. Eh, well, he rained not of the whole of the whole—*du tout*

LOCAL

SUNDAY MORNING

Tourist (staying at the Glenmulctem Hotel—dubiously). "Can I—ah—have a boat?"

Boatman. "Oo—aye!"

Tourist. "But I thought you—ah—never broke the—aw—Sabbath in Scotland?"

Boatman. "Aweel, ye ken the Sawbath disna' come doon to the loch—it just staps at the hottle!"

"CANNY"

Sister. "Why, Charles, you've got raw whiskey here!"
Charles. "Well, it's hardly worth while to bring water. We can always find that as we go along—when we want it."

du tout !   Il faisait un temps superbe—he was
making a superb time, the route was well agreeable, and the voyage lasted but two hours, and
not twelve. What droll of idea! In scottish *twa*
is two, not twelve. I was so content to arrive so
quick, and without to be wetted that I gave the
coacher a good to-drink — *un bon pourboire* —
though before to start all the voyagers had paid
him a "tipp," that which he called a "driver's
fee." Again what droll of idea! To give the
to-drink before to start, and each one the same—
six pennys.

My friend encountered me and conducted me
to his house, where I have passed fifteen days, a
sojourn of the most agreeables. And all the time
almost not one sole drop of rain! *J'avais beau*
—I had fine—to buy all my impermeable vestments, I carry them never. One sole umbrella
suffices me, and I open him but two times. And
yet one says that the Scotland is a rainy country.
It is perhaps a season *tout à fait*—all to fact—
exceptional. But fifteen days almost without
rain! One would believe himself at the border
of the Mediterranean, absolutely at the South.

CAUTIOUS

Visitor (at out-of-the-way inn in the North). " Do you know anything about salmon-poaching in this neighbourhood ? "

Landlady (whose son is not above suspicion).—" Eh—no, sir. Maybe it's a new style of cooking as we haven't heard of in these parts, as you see, sir, we only do our eggs that way ; and "—*(brightening up)*—" if you like 'em, I can get you a dish at once ! "

And I have eaten of the "porridg," me Auguste! *Partout* I essay the dish of the country. I take at first a spoonful pure and simple. *Oh la, la!* My friend offers me of the cream. It is well. Also of the salt. *Quelle idée!* But no, before me I perceive a dish of *confiture*, that which the scottish call "marmaladde." *A la bonne heure!* With some marmaladde, some

A DECIDED OPINION

Proprietor of shootings ("*in the course of conversation*"). "Yes, but you know, Sandy, it's difficult to choose between the Scylla of a shy tenant, and the Charybdis of——"

Sandy (*promptly*). "Aweel! Gie me the siller, an' any-buddy that likes may hae the tither!"

Chappie (after missing his fourth stag, explains). " Aw—fact is, the—aw—waving grass was in my way."

Old Stalker. " Hoot, mon, wad he hae me bring out a scythe ?"

cream, and much of sugar, I find that the " porridg " is enough well, for I taste him no more.

One day we make an ascension, and we see many grouses. Only we can not to shoot, for it is not yet the season of the huntings. It is but a hill that we mount. The name appears me to be french, but bad written. " Ben Venue," that is to say, " *Bienvenu* "—*soyez le bienvenu.* She is one of the first of the scottish hills, and she says

Our artist catches it again this winter in the Highlands.

A FINE HEAD (BUT NOT OF THE RIGHT SORT OF CATTLE)

Perkins has paid a mint of money for his shooting, and has had bad luck all the season. To-day, however, he gets a shot, only—it turns out to be at a cow!

"welcome" in french. It is a pretty idea, and a politeness very amiable towards my country. I salute the hospitable Scotland and I thank her. It is a great country, of brave men, of charming women—ah, I recall to myself some eyes so beautiful, some forms so attracting!—of ravishing landscapes, and, at that epoch there, of a climate so delicious. She has one sole and one great defect. The best scottish hotels cost very dear, and, my

A "SCENE" IN THE HIGHLANDS

Ill-used husband (under the bed). "Aye! Ye may crack me, and ye may thrash me, but ye canna break my manly sperrit. I'll na come oot!!"

MR. PUNCH IN THE HIGHLANDS

He is at present on a boating excursion, and describes the motion as extremely
pleasant, and has no dread of sea-sickness.

faith, the two or three that I visited are not great thing like comfortable—*ne sont pas grand'chose comme comfortable !*

One day we make a little excursion on the Lake of Lomond. The lake is well beautiful, and the steamboat is excellent. But in one certain hotel, in descending from a *breack*, and before to embark, we take the " lunch." We bargain not, we ask not even the price, we eat at the *table d'hôte* like all the world in Swiss, in France, even in Germany, when there is but one half hour before the departure of the train or of the boat. *Oh la, la !* I have eaten in the spanish hotels, on the steamboats of the italian lakes, even in the *restaurants—mon Dieu !*—of the english railways, but never, never— *au grand jamais*—have I eaten a *déjeuner* like that ! One dish I shall forget never ; some exterior green leaves of lettuce, without oil or vinegar, which they called a " salad." *Parbleu*—by blue ! In all the history of the world there has been but one man who would have could to eat her with pleasure—Nabuchodonosor !

Agree, &c.,

AUGUSTE.

"GAME" IN THE HIGHLANDS

Captain Jinks. "Birds plentiful, I hope, Donald?"
Donald. "Tousans, sir—in tousans."
Captain J. "Any zebras?"
Donald (anxious to please). "Is't zebras? They're in tousans, too."
Captain J. "And gorillas, no doubt?"
Donald. "Well, noo an' then we see ane or twa—just like yersel'."

173

MISS LAVINIA BROUNJONES'S ADVENTURES
IN THE HIGHLANDS
Lavinia takes a siesta,

And the frightful situation she finds herself in at the end
of it.

Lavinia arrives at a waterfall, and asks its name. The shepherd (not understanding English) informs her in Gaelic that it is called (as Lavinia supposes) "Vicharoobashal-lochoggilnabo." Lavinia thinks it a very pretty name.

A bright idea strikes the shepherd, and before Lavinia can remonstrate, he transports her, in the usual manner, to the other side.

MISS **LAVINIA BROUNJONES**

She comes suddenly on a strange structure—apparently
a native fort, and is just going to sketch it, when a savage
of gigantic stature, and armed to the teeth, starts from an
ambush, and menaces her in Gaelic!

TWENTY HOURS AFTER

EUSTON, 8 P.M.

I'M sick of this sweltering weather.
Phew! ninety degrees in the shade!
I long for the hills and the heather,
I long for the kilt and the plaid;
I long to escape from this hot land
Where there isn't a mouthful of air,
And fly to the breezes of Scotland—
It's never too stuffy up there.

OVERHEARD IN THE HIGHLANDS

First Chieftain. "I say, old chap, what a doose of a bore these games are!"

Second Chieftain. "Ah, but, my dear boy, it is this sort of thing that has made us Scotchmen *what we are!!*"

For weeks I have sat in pyjamas,
  And found even these were *de trop*,
And envied the folk of Bahamas
  Who dress in a feather or so ;
But now there's an end to my grilling,
  My Inferno's a thing of the past ;
Hurrah ! there's the whistle a-shrilling—
  We are off to the Highlands at last !

"SERMONS IN STONES"

Tourist (of an inquiring and antiquarian turn). " Now I suppose, farmer, that large cairn of stones has some history ?"

Highland Farmer. " Ooh, aye, that buig o' stanes has a gran' history whatever ! "

Tourist (eagerly). " Indeed ! I should like to——What is the legend——? "

Farmer. " Just a gran' history ! " (*Solemnly.*) " It took a' ma cairts full and horses sax months to gather them aff the land and pit them ther-r-re !! "

JETSAM AND FLOTSAM

Smith being shut out from the Continent this year, takes a cottage ornée on Dee-Side, Scotland. The children are sent up first. The house is described as "conveniently furnished"—they find it so!

M 2

CALLANDER, 4 P.M.

The dull leaden skies are all clouded
In the gloom of a sad weeping day,
The desolate mountains are shrouded
In palls of funereal grey ;
'Mid the skirl of the wild wintry weather
The torrents descend in a sheet
As we shiver all huddled together
In the reek of the smouldering peat.

A plague on the Highlands! to think of
The heat that but lately we banned ;
Oh ! what would we give for a blink of
The bright sunny side of the Strand !
To think there are folk that still revel
In Summer, and fling themselves down,
In the Park, or St. James ? What the d——
Possessed us to hurry from town ?

"OUT OF TUNE AND HARSH." — *First Elder*
(*at the Kirk* " *Skellin'* "). " Did ye hear Dougal
More snorin' in the sermon ? " *Second Elder.*
" Parefec'ly disgracefu' ! He's waukened 's a' ! "

IN THE WILDS OF THE NORTH.

Hungry Saxon (just arrived, with equally hungry family). " Well, now—er—what can you give us for dinner, as soon as we've had a wash ? "

Scotch Lassie. " Oh, jist onything ! "

H. S. (rubbing his hands in anticipation). " Ah ! Now we'll have a nice juicy steak."

Lassie. " A—weel. We'll be haein' some steak here maybe by the boat i' the morn's morn ! "

H. S. (a little crestfallen). " Oh—well—chops then. We'll say mutton chops."

Lassie. " Oh, ay, but we've no been killin' a sheep the day ! " [*Ends up with boiled eggs, and vows to remain at home for the future.*

THE DUKE OF ATHOLL'S SHILLING (1851)

THE *North British Mail* assures us that the Duke of Atholl exacts one shilling a head from every person taking a walk in his ground at Dunkeld. This is rather dear; but the impost would be insupportable if his Grace insisted upon also showing himself for the money.

A HIGHLAND CORONACH

(Or Lament over the Acts and State of the Duke of Atholl.
After Scott.

> HE has shut up the mountain,
> He has locked up the forest,
> He has bunged up the fountain,
> When our need was the sorest;
> The traveller stirring
> To the North, may dogs borrow;
> But the Duke gives no hearing,
> No pass—but to sorrow.
>
> The hand of the tourist
> Grasps the carpet-bag grimly,
> But a face of the dourest
> Frowns through the Glen dimly.

182

The autumn winds, rushing,
Stir a kilt of the queerest,
Duke and gillies come crushing
Where pleasure is nearest !

Queer foot on the corrie,
Oddly loving to cumber—
Give up this odd foray,
Awake from your slumber !
Take your ban from the mountain,
Take your lock from the river,
Take your bolt from the fountain,
Now at once, and for ever !

The sad fate of our only ham.—The pursuit.

A RARA MONGRELLIS

Tourist. "Your dog appears to be deaf, as he pays no attention to me."

Shepherd. "Na, na, sir. She's a varra wise dog, for all tat. But she only speaks Gaelic."

"IN FOR IT"

Innocent Tourist. "No fish to be caught in Loch Fine now? And how do you support yourself?"

Native. "Whiles she carries parcels, and whiles she raws people in ta poat, and whiles a shentleman 'ull give her a saxpence or a shillin'!"

A BLANK DAY

The Keeper (to Brown, who rents the forest). "Doon wi' ye! Doon wi' ye! Get ahint a stang!"

Brown (out of temper—he had been "stalking" about all the morning, and missed several times). "Yes, it's all very well to say 'Get behind a stone.' But show me one!!"—show me one!!"

The Laird, as a delicate compliment, serenades him.

Mr. Punch passes a night at McGillie Cullum Castle.

A BAD SEASON

Sportsman. "I can assure you, what with the rent of the moor, and my expenses, and 'what not,' the birds have cost me—ah—a sovereign apiece!!"

Keeper. "A' weel, sir! 'Deed it's a maircy ye didna kill na mair o' 'em!!"

188

CANDID

Sportsman. "Boy, you've been at this whiskey!"
Boy (who has brought the luncheon-basket). "Na! The cooark wadna come oot!"

"UNCO CANNY"

Noble Sportsman. "Missed, eh?"
Cautious Keeper. "Weel, a' wadna gang quite sae faur
as to say that; but a' doot ye hav'na *exactly* hit."

THE SONG OF THE SCOTCH TOURIST

Those Scotch hotels! Those Scotch hotels
Are fit for princes and for swells;
But their high charges don't agree
With humbler travellers like me.

Twelve shillings daily for my board
Is more than I can well afford,
For this includes nor ale nor wine,
Whereof I drink some when I dine.

Bad sherry's charged at eight-and-six,
A price that in my gizzard sticks:
And if I want a pint of port,
A crown is what I'm pilfer'd for 't.

For service, too, I have to pay,
Two shillings, as a rule, per day:

A VERY DIFFERENT MATTER

Southern Lord (staying at Highland castle). "Thank you so much. I—ah—weally enjoy your music. I think of having a piper at my own place."

Sandy the piper. "An' fat kin' o' a piper would your lordship be needin' ? "

Southern Lord. "Oh, certainly a good piper like yourself, Sandy."

Sandy (sniffing). "Och! Inteet!—Ye might easily fin' a lord like your lordship, but it's nae sae easy to fin' a piper like me whatever ! "

Mr. Punch in the Highlands

> Yet always, when I leave the door,
> The boots and waiter beg for more.
>
> So, till a fortune I can spend,
> Abroad my autumn steps I'll bend;
> Far cheaper there, experience tells,
> Is living than at Scotch hotels!

THE END

BRADBURY, AGNEW, & CO. LD., PRINTERS, LONDON AND TONBRIDGE.